MW01180788

Kids in Their Communities™

I Live on an Island

Stasia Ward Kehoe

The Rosen Publishing Group's
PowerKids Press™
New York

For Kevin, Thomas, and Mak

Published in 2000 by The Rosen Publishing Group, Inc.
29 East 21st Street, New York, NY 10010

First Edition

Book Design: Michael de Guzman

Photo Credits and Photo Illustrations: pp. 4, 7, 8, 12, 15, 16, 19, 20 by Clayton Davis; p. 11 CORBIS/Lowell Georgia.

Kehoe, Stasia Ward, 1968–
        I live on an island / Stasia Ward Kehoe
        p. cm — (Kids in their communities)
    SUMMARY: Nine-year-old Lindsey describes her life on an island off the coast of Virginia including her home, ways of getting around, prevalence of seafood, and the natural wildlife.
        ISBN 0-8239-5439-0
        1. Chincoteague Island (Va.) — Social life and customs Juvenile literature. 2. Children—Virginia—Chincoteague Island—Social life and customs Juvenile literature. [1. Chincoteague Island (Va.)—Social life and customs. 2. Virginia—Social life and customs.] I. Title. II. Series: Kehoe, Stasia Ward, 1968– Kids in their communities.
    F232.A2 K45 1999
    975.5'16—dc21   99-26369
                                                                            CIP

Manufactured in the United States of America

CONTENTS

Lindsey

My name is Lindsey. I am nine years old. I live with my family on the island of Chincoteague off the coast of Virginia. An island is a body of land that has water all around it. The water to the east of Chincoteague is called Chincoteague Bay. The water to the west of Chincoteague is called the Assateague Channel. On the other side of this narrow channel is Assateague Island.

◀ *I like to sit on my front steps and enjoy the island breeze.*

Island Homes

My house has an upstairs and a downstairs, a playroom, and an attic. There are many different kinds of houses on the island. People live in ranch-style homes, cottages, and small, two-story houses. Some homes are built on stilts, or posts, so that the water does not get inside when the island floods. In bad weather the water around the island can **overflow** onto the land, so the stilts are important to keep houses safe and dry.

My house is also a bed-and-breakfast, which means it is like a small hotel where island visitors can stay. ▶

Getting Around

Chincoteague is a small island, seven miles long and one-and-a-half miles wide. It is easy to ride your bicycle almost anywhere you want to go. You need a car if you want to drive over the bridge to get to the shopping malls, doctors' offices, movie theaters, or other places on the **mainland**. Lots of my friends' parents own boats. They use them to travel between Chincoteague and Assateague Islands or as another way to get to the mainland.

◀ *It can be fun to look at the boats in the harbor.*

The Sea

Lots of people on the island make their living from the sea. They work as fishermen or fisherwomen, boatbuilders, and artists. The artists do paintings and sculptures of sea creatures and the sea. Almost everyone on the island eats a lot of seafood.

Chincoteague is famous for its clam **shoals** and oyster beds. An Oyster Festival is held here each October. Oysters taste good steamed, **raw**, and lots of other ways!

"Shucking" oysters means taking the oysters out of their shells. ▶

School

I am in the third grade at school. There is one book every kid in my school has read or heard about. The book is called *Misty of Chincoteague*. A woman named Marguerite Henry wrote it in 1947. It is the story of two children who **tame** a wild pony. The book won many prizes. It was even made into a movie! *Misty of Chincoteague* helped to make our island world-famous.

 I like to visit the statue of Misty.

The Volunteer Fire Department and the Ponies

Misty was based on a real pony, who was in a special Chincoteague Island event called the "Pony Penning." In May of 1924, after two bad fires on the island, a group of men organized the Chincoteague Volunteer Fire Department. To raise money, they held a Pony Penning Day. This event still happens today. Volunteer firefighters round up wild ponies on Assateague Island and swim them across the channel for an **auction** on Chincoteague.

People from around the world come to Chincoteague for the Volunteer Fire Department's Pony Penning each July. ▶

14

Wildlife

Assateague Island, just across the Assateague Channel from Chincoteague, is home to many **endangered species**, like the Delmarva Peninsula fox squirrel and the piping plover. Over 300 species of birds visit the island, too. In the fall, you can see Canada geese, snow geese, and tundra swans. Assateague has over 30 miles of beaches so there is plenty of room for the wild ponies to run free. The island also has **marshes**, **loblolly** pine forests, and sand dunes.

◀ *I like to stand on the dock to watch for birds.*

Seashells

I love to visit the beautiful beaches of Assateague Island. Sometimes Mom, Dad, and I take a boat over to the island. There are lots of shells on the ground in some places. It is a good idea to wear shoes so that you do not cut your feet. You can see lots of different kinds of shells on the island. The shells have pretty names like Angel Wing, Atlantic Moon Shell, and Slipper Shell. Lots of shells are named for the shape or thing they look like.

It is fine to look at shells, but there are special rules about collecting shells on Assateague Island. ▶

Tourists

In the summer and fall, many **tourists** come to Chincoteague. Some come for the Pony Penning. Others come for the Oyster Festival, art shows, and bird-watching. Chincoteague is different when the tourists come. The beaches get crowded. You have to wait in a line to eat in restaurants. Tourism helps the people of Chincoteague earn money. Still, it is nice when the tourists go home and island life gets quiet again.

 Fishing is one of the things that brings tourists to Chincoteague.

Island Life

Mom took me to visit New York City last fall. It was full of tall buildings and busy people. I had fun, but I would rather be at home on Chincoteague Island. Things move a little more slowly on our island and there's lots of nature everywhere. I hope I always live on Chincoteauge island!

Glossary

auction (AWK-shun) When objects or animals are sold to the person who offers the highest amount of money.

endangered (in-DAYN-jurd) When something is in danger of no longer existing.

loblolly (LAHB-lah-lee) A pine tree of the southeastern United States with flaky bark, long needles, and cones.

mainland (MAYN-land) Nearby land area where people from an island get supplies not available on the island.

marshes (MAR-shiz) Areas of soft, wet land.

overflow (oh-vur-FLOH) To run outside of, or above, boundaries.

raw (RAW) Uncooked.

shoals (SHOWLZ) A large group of sea creatures, like clams.

species (SPEE-sheez) A group of animals that are very much alike.

tame (TAYM) To make a wild person, animal, or thing gentle.

tourists (TUR-ists) People visiting a place where they do not live.

Index

Web Sites:

To learn more about Chincoteague Island, check out this Web site:

http://www.chincoteague.com/index.html